365 Days...
with my
curious
Cat

Pam Brown

photography by Yoneo Morita

MJF BOOKS | New York

Published by MJF Books
Fine Communications
589 Eighth Avenue, 6th Floor
New York, NY 10018

365 Days with My Curious Cat
LC Control Number: 2018945259

ISBN 978-1-60671-429-4

Photography copyright © 2012 by Yoneo Morita/Hanadeka™
Words by Pam Brown copyright © 2016 by Helen Exley Creative Ltd.
Selection and arrangement copyright © 2016
by Helen Exley Creative Ltd.

This edition is published by MJF Books
in arrangement with Exley Publications Ltd.

Printed in China.

MJF Books and the MJF colophon are trademarks
of Fine Creative Media, Inc.

[1010]   10 9 8 7 6 5 4 3 2 1

There is nothing so beautiful
as a sleeping cat.

Dear cats.

Dear best of friends.

There is always a little
lost cat waiting to
fill the gap in
your life.

So small — so full
of love and ingenuity.
So frail — so full of life.

Every tiny
bundle of fur is
fully armed.

A dog looks guilty
if he's sinned.
A cat, never.

Tread softly.
The cat's asleep.

A little cat
has taught many a child
to care, to love.

A cat brings
beauty into the
dullest day.

All cats — from Bengal tigers to alley cats — are variations on a single splendid theme.

A little cat brings
the jungle into
suburbia.

A cat purring
soothes the most
troubled heart.

A cat is loyal.

But not very.

Every cat is
feral under
the skin.

A cat obeys rules.

His.

One owns a dog.
One cooperates
with a cat.

A dog who has broken something
is full of regret and
apology.

A cat swears he was never
near the thing.

People are usually honored
when a cat decides
to like them.

A cat is an enigma.

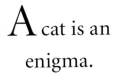

Cat long since
achieved perfection
— and sees no reason for
further adjustment.

Try to learn Cat.
It is a subtle language
but well worth the effort.

A dog secretly hopes that one day
he will become human.
A cat would be appalled
by the possibility.

Even the most sedate cat
sometimes indulges in a
silly half hour.

Owner? Mistress? Master?
Nothing applies.

Slave comes near it.

A cat has mastered conservation of energy. If nothing demands his immediate attention

— he simply switches off.

A cat will accept you
as companion and provider.
But not as his superior.

Those who love cats tickle, stroke, rub, and snuggle on request. But warily.

A cat loves you
after his fashion.
He does not
worship you.

When someone,
through age or loneliness
or grief, finds love has left them,
they can often rediscover
it in a little cat.

Search a room
from top to
bottom for your
missing cat.
Pause.
And your
cat will stroll
out of it with
a supercilious
smile on his face.

We learned
lateral thinking
from cats.

To laugh at a cat who has missed his footing is to mortally offend him.

The love of a little cat should
never be despised.

A cat knows very well what Go, Come, Stay mean. He simply refuses to acknowledge them as applying to himself.
A cat gives instructions. He does not take them.

A cat is full of opinions.

But he keeps them to himself.

The human heart clings to a
fragile hope that we will find
each other in eternity.

Warn a visitor that your cat can be downright dangerous if he is picked up; turn away, and subsequently you will find him curled in her arms, eyes blissfully closed, and purring ecstatically.

Scold a dog and he cowers.
Scold a cat and he washes his paws.

A cat refuses to be bored. He will either invent a game or sleep.

A cat hates above any
other thing making
a fool of itself.

A cat does not need to demonstrate his affection wildly. A leaning against your legs. A chirrup. A gentle paw. "I'm glad you're home."

With dogs you know exactly
where you stand.
With a cat?
Never.

There is enough of the wild left in both cats and dogs to justify a little caution.

No cat ever has a Bad Hair Day.

The oldest,
ugliest, smelliest
cat can often
be the most loving.

A cat adjusts his demands according to the gullibility of his human.

People of importance
often turn to cats.
They neither
flatter nor fawn.

People who need to be
worshipped should not
choose a cat.

A cat who doesn't
want to be found
isn't.

Even the most
sober-minded cat cannot
resist a moving blob
of light.

When your cat is sulking,

steer clear.

A cat understands most
of what you say — but he finds
it judicious to pretend
that he doesn't.

A cat is perfectly willing
to fit into your ways —
providing he can
retain his own.

The most devoted cat owner lives uneasily with the suspicion that his cat knows more than he cares to admit.

A cat keeps its secrets safe.

One resents being under another's thumb, but one accepts being under a paw.

"Heel!" says the dog owner.
And, with luck, is obeyed.
"Don't be ridiculous,"
says cat.

A cat needs no words — the touch of a little paw — a whiskery kiss — a drowsy purr are enough to tell you that he loves you.

Time passes. Things change. Says
cat, I let the current take me where it
will — and so remain content.

Owners say their dogs are almost human. A cat would be appalled.

A cat does
what he planned
to do.

A cat is a small perfection.

And knows it.

A cat very quietly reorganizes your existence.

No cat is wholly domesticated.
Some fraction of his being will
always be wild. And this is why we
cherish him.

A cat that is looking especially angelic is up to something.

A cat rearranges your life to
suit his own.

A cat has preferences.
He will let you know.

One never quite gets over
the loss of cat.

Play a game with your cat.

By his rules.

Go away, says cat. I am concentrating. I aim to achieve the ultimate in sleep.

One never takes a cat for a walk.
He may, of course, choose to
accompany you.

Store the Christmas turkey in the downstairs bathroom for safety. Two hours later open the door to release a happy cat and a legless bird.

A cat never admits defeat.
He just pretends he wasn't
really interested in
the first place.

A cat never examines his conscience. He has none.

A cat has his reasons, which he's not going to explain.

A dog dances with delight at the sight of its master, barks, leaps, scampers, rolls over, nuzzles, drools.

A cat gives a restrained hello.

A cat puts aside
yesterday and does not
plan for his tomorrow.
He very wisely lives
simply for today.

A cat who stares at you for any length of time is plotting something.

Prepare.

Over the centuries we have changed — in habits, clothing, and belief — but cat is constant. Riding the pharaoh's punt through tall papyrus stems. Sprawled across a papal knee. Sleeping beside an open kitchen fire. Bright-eyed in candlelight. They reach soft paws to us across the years. Our dear familiar friends.

A cat needs no tricks to demand
attention. He is simply There.

Try dominating a cat,
and he'll leave home.

No cat belongs completely to any human being — a companion but never a possession.

We moved. People phone. Always
to ask after the cat.

A cat outlives a flower, a mouse, a summer. But never long enough. The heart still yearns for him long after he has gone.

The laws of physics
do not apply
to cats.

Those who require obedience
should not acquire a cat.

Tickle my tummy. Stroke my lovely fur. Delight in my waving paws, my reverberating song. And I will clamp you. And bite you to the bone.

A cat has a rich vocabulary, but we are too ignorant to understand.

A bored cat is a restless cat —
looking for trouble.

A cat knows what he knows but is not going to let you know it.

Every cat, pampered or scruffy, stray or sheltered, is utterly unique and worthy of respect.

Canned fish.

No.

Fresh salmon,

yes.

Call a dog and he comes. Call a cat and he may. Eventually.

There is nothing so laid back as a
laid-back cat.

A cat can beg, implore, beseech
without twitching a whisker.

A cat has an infinite ability to make one feel guilty.

We can rarely guess what a cat is thinking.

Maybe it's just as well.

Cat lovers bear the scars.

A cat lover finds friends
the world over.

A cat is wiser than he wants
you to recognize.

A dog gobbles. A cat picks, savors,
and delivers judgment.

A cat is never lost for something to do. He can always sleep.

What is a cat? Anything that he
decides to be.

A cat doesn't bark or wag or
scrabble when he wants out.
He simply sits and
stares at you.

A cat agrees to live with you — on his terms.

You're never done with a cat. He sees to that.

"Who's a lovely boy, then?"
And the dog rolls over in delight.
The cat gives a withering look
and leaves.

There is no such thing as a cat owner.

No cat is the same as any other.

No cat cares to explain what he wants. He lets you work it out.

A hungry cat is an insistent cat.

A cat sprawled on its back is waiting hopefully for someone to pause and rub his tummy.

We mourn the loss of our cats. For they were our companions. Part of our lives. Bound to us by love. A little of the heartbreak will stay with us forever. A little of the joy we knew together.

Every movement a cat makes has
been perfected through millennia.
And he knows it.

"Nine out of ten cats adore
this food," they say.
Me, I'm the one
that doesn't.

A cat cannot speak
— but he can still
give orders.

A cat can be obedient if
it suits him.

It usually doesn't.

There are a thousand kinds of Dog. There is one Cat.

Cats only relish the highlights of
their day. Food, cuddles, hunting,
washing, play. And sleep
the rest away.

Backs to the wall. The cat is in galloping mode.

A dog loves to be laughed at. A cat takes a long while to forgive you.

Cat. Remember me. Come home.

A kitten believes all things are permissible so long as they are fun.

The most blasé and sophisticated cat cannot resist a blob of light that moves across the wall. And careers around the room swatting the uncatchable.

Cats, you must realize,
have quietly taken
over the world.

Cats are masters of the art of infiltration.

"As helpless as a kitten"
is a nonsense.
Kittens cope.

To a dog, dinner is dinner.
To a cat it is a source of
amusement and invention.

A dog forgives his tormentors.
A cat never quite forgets.

A cat can learn a multitude of skills if it suits him.

"Ah," say the dog owners.
"He's nearly human."
Cat owners would not dare.

A very small cat can dominate a household.

A dog performs to delight his owner, a cat to delight himself.

Try me on a leash?

Don't be ridiculous.

A cat can outthink and outmaneuver any human being.

A reformed street cat can be the sweetest natured of them all.

A cat eats, sleeps, sits, and stares and suddenly erupts into ingenious mischief.

Unfortunately, cats have never faced the fact that humans have no fur or that play fights draw blood. And indignation.

Cats make a specialty of hiding in places they could not possibly get into.

To some blind souls all cats are much alike. To a cat lover every cat from the beginning of time has been utterly and amazingly unique.

The most cushiony, comfortable, contented cat lies with its eyes half closed, its paws doubled neatly beneath its chest, and sings.

It doesn't matter if you are six feet four and broad of shoulder; if a kitten is looking for a mother-figure, you're it.

Human beings are drawn to cats because they are all we are not — self-contained, elegant in everything they do, relaxed, assured.

Cats are mysterious, elegant, beautiful. Cats are ridiculous, unpredictable…and deeply disobedient. They love as they choose to love. Cats are who they decide to be.

Perfectly sensible people
apologize to cats.

An ecstatic cat, welcoming you home, can purr so loudly it makes you laugh out loud with joy.

Dear cat, exasperating cat, we love you. We turn to you in sadness, in loneliness, in sickness. Dear cat. Dear comfort. Dear friend.

Cats know, quietly and with complete conviction, that they are the superior species.

Do not confuse the implements in your cat's feet with simple claws. They are excavators, stilettos, slings, lancets, rippers of curtains, engravers of furniture.

A cat asleep
in the garden
is wrapped
around in scent
and birdsong.

Cat has always known his lineage was more distinguished than that of any pharaoh. And has lived his life accordingly.

A cat could talk if he wanted to.

But he doesn't.

Cat owners spend
most of their days
trying to outthink
their cats.

How small a creature to hold
one's heart.

The beauties of an ordinary cat can fill a drowsy afternoon with wonder. No need for long safaris — the marvel purrs upon your lap.

To possess a cat is to be a part of
a worldwide company of
devoted slaves.

Cats wrap themselves
in summer as in
a coverlet.

Cat owners sometimes have an ugly suspicion that the Lord of the Universe has whiskers and a long, ginger tail.

A cat expects a chair at the dinner table.

Especially if it's formal.

A cat never ceases to be astounded by your stupidity. After all, he has explained a dozen times how to open the back door.

I don't think the word "relax"
was invented until the
discovery of
The Cat.

The loss of a cat never quite heals.

Albert moved in after having explored the possibilities of most other houses on the street. Good garden, a woman who was obviously a kindly, easily persuaded soul.

A cat is of course capable of
remarkable feats

but prefers
not to
pursue
them.

One small cat changes
coming home to an empty house
into coming home.

A cat's paw is built for flicking.
Food pellets. Water. Clocks. Vases.
The contents of a pantry.

A cross kitten comes across the room, burning with rage — his fur on end. At all costs do not laugh at him. A kitten has his pride.

You own a dog but
you feed a cat.

How good it is to live with a cat —
for a cat does not look for perfection,
only food, shelter, a cuddle when he
needs it, and someone adept
at stroking.

A bored cat, a restless cat.
Or asleep.

All kittens set out to teach their humans to adapt to the needs of a cat. As a reward, they grant them the position of honorary cat.

A richly contented purr can drown out the radio.

A cat is the bridge that links us to the wild wood and the time beyond time.

No, says Cat, you've moved my bed.
I do not like that chicken.
I've lost my appetite.
I know I liked
it last week.
But now?
No.

After scolding one's cat one looks into his face and is seized by the ugly suspicion that he understood every word. And has filed it for reference.

Never let a cat near a man
with a wig.

For a kitten the world
is an enchantment.
A challenge.

At best, one is one's cat's companion. At worst, its slave.

Try to photograph a cat and he will present the back of his head. Until you've worn down the battery, when he will immediately perform.

A cat has a very short attention
span unless he's watching
a mouse hole.

A lost dog is a pitiable, bewildered creature. Poor soul.

A lost cat is looking for an alternative residence.

Cat's claws were given to it to hunt, to fight, and to climb trees, but centuries have extended its abilities to shinny up curtains, open doors, lift lids, and rearrange the ornaments.

Dancers watch cats, and
sigh with envy.

A cat may have a limited vocabulary, but it can tell you exactly what it wants, and will accept no excuses whatsoever.

He is a kindly cat, loving beyond reason; head-butter, nuzzler, fluffy sprawl of fur; belly spread, he lies like an upturned table, forepaws kneading, demanding notice and a tummy rub.

When the heart is desolate, a little cat will warm and comfort it.

Even Fabergé could never have fashioned something as exquisite in its detail as a tiny kitten.

The physicists are confronted with two great mysteries: black holes, and how a cat can be in two places at once.

"Come," says master — and the dog comes. "Go," he says — and the dog goes. Use your entire vocabulary on a cat and he will do exactly as he pleases.

You have been calling the cat for twenty minutes. He is sitting three yards from you in the shelter of a bush. Amused.

A small cat stretches out its paw
to touch your face and you are no
longer lost or lonely.

The shabbiest cat
has the mark of ancient
royalty about him.

A cat believes in privacy.

His. Not yours.

Cats give us life. Sleeping, tuning their heartbeats to our own, singing away sorrow, unraveling the day.

Kittens undermine pomposity.

In midchase she stops. Sits. Washes her feet. Stares at you with disapproval. "For heaven's sake, woman," she declares. "Act your age."

A cat loves to help you
tidy your papers.

The possession of a cat
links mankind the
whole world over.

A cat deflates
the largest ego by merely
narrowing its eyes.

Even the most sober-minded cat is capable of a Funny Half Hour.

Dogs live with you;
cats board with you.

Never give your friend's cat the food your cat won't eat. Give it two weeks and he'll eat nothing else.

A cat who doesn't want to, won't.

Cats bring the scent of summer
home on their fur.

Only those who do not have a cat
say that cats can't talk.

So small a creature to make so great
a difference to your life.

Cats arrange themselves to present
the best effect.

The most gentle cat has a shocking range of swear words in his vocabulary.

A cat stalks into the living room.
"Put down everything.
It's time to play."

A cat is never bored. At a loose end he will remove all the keys from their hooks, climb the north face of the bookcase, or eat the rubber plant.

A cat loves to hear you calling its name. It will listen contentedly for an hour at a stretch. Of course, it won't respond — only listen.

Old ladies, after a lifetime of dealing with people, find the company of cats a great relief. Cats are companionable and kind, courteous in their dictatorial demands, delicate in their greed, clean, beautiful, and elegant… and as vulnerable as we all are.

A pup likes to be laughed at. The smallest kitten is mortally offended.

The agitated meow, the frantic meow, is "You've been out for hours, and look, my bowl is empty!"

Many an ancient tomcat has a kitten's heart.

Cats have never yet grasped the concept of No.

If a cat is disgusted, it's no good tempting it with a twitching string. You are inviting a look of withering disdain that would sit well on a duchess.

Who needs TV when there's
a kitten around?

Any cat knows the precise cost of every form of cat food and chooses, unfailingly, the most expensive.

There are quiet, shy, gentle kittens, and comic, bold-as-brass kittens. All beautiful. And all needing a human being who will think them the very best kitten in the universe.

There is nothing so asleep
as a kitten.

There is nothing so off-putting as an exasperated kitten who has failed to explain something to you, despite putting it in words of one syllable.

How airily our cats summon and dismiss us. And we obey.

Mankind takes itself too seriously.
Kittens are a most effective cure.

"Can't you see it? Can't you smell it? Can't you hear it?" the little cat asks. And regretfully we shake our heads.

A cat needs to touch you now and then for reassurance.

A cat gets what he wants.

Cats bring a little magic to the dullest life. A little mystery. The scent of wild green places, of darkness and adventure.

A cat will show its outer beauty to the world and perhaps hint at its affectionate heart. All else is hidden, kept for the one it loves.

No need to watch oneself, or act a part. One's cat knows one is fairly stupid — but doesn't mind.

How comforting the gentle snoring
of a little cat.

A dog will pursue a thrown ball, and bring it back. A cat will sit under a chair, swipe the ball — and let the thrower retrieve it.

A dog goes on loving, however he is treated. A cat walks out and finds another home.

A cat will imagine a piece of paper on a string to be a mouse, until you enter into the spirit of the game. It will then regard you as a lunatic, and take to washing its feet.

You may love me, says cat.
On my terms.

The cat stands in the doorway. "Come. At once. I need the tap turned on."

A kitten brings a joy out of all
proportion to its size.

Kittens take us in hand very soon in their lives. They summon us to play. They sulk if put down from our knees. They hog the bed.

Stop scratching your cat for one
moment and a single paw reaches out
and reminds you to resume.

I call into the night. He sits in shadow and listens. Appreciating my anxiety. Biding his time.

No cat is as virtuous as he looks.

A cat means to do everything with elegance and is horribly embarrassed if he fails.

The gentle touch of an outstretched paw. The butt of a head…the trust and affection of a little cat.

It is good to keep a cat. They force us to realize we are not the only reality.

We play together. Doze away the summer afternoons together. Rest in a shared contentment. You are part of our family — what would we do without you?

We hold every cat that we have ever
had safe in our hearts forever.

All treasured. All mourned, however long or short their existence. The imprint cats leave on the years can never be erased.

She has no words, but by small touchings and buttings, she shows her love for you and tries to distract you from your sorrow.

Kit, Katten, Cat.
Charm. Mischief. Wisdom.

One never ceases to find new wonders in a cat. Pattern and swirl of fur, elegance of movement, perfection of form. Delicacy of whisker, brilliance of eye, gentleness of outstretched paw and loving, butting head. Expressiveness of tail. Complexity of ear. A mouth of pink and ivory, curved tongue and shining teeth. A voice of mystery.

We seek beauty, poise, grace, elegance. The cat does not. He has them already.

Come to your call? says cat. Don't be ridiculous. I have my self-respect.

Turn away if your cat jumps short, and hide your smile. No animal can be so deeply offended as a cat.

A cat is always on the wrong side
of any door.

Cats don't see why they should waste time learning words. After all — they have no intention of obeying anyone.

A great many cats have, unknown to their official owners, several names — given by neighbors who have been hoodwinked into believing they are sad little strays.

Round, misty-blue eyes stare desperately. Love me, they say, let me into your life — so that I can begin to take over your entire existence.

Dogs on the whole are honest,
even showing guilt.

Cats lie habitually.

Anywhere in the world you can find someone to Talk Cat with.

Live by his rules and you and the cat will get along very well.

The words
No, Get down,
Stop, Leave it,
mean nothing
to a cat.

The tiger is undoubtedly the most beautiful animal on the planet. Your tabby Tom, of course, comes a close second.

Cat says: Now is the time for stillness. Gentle my fur and I will sing for you. And my song will soothe your heart to quietness.

A cat's gaze has a quietness that
calms the human heart.

Centuries of practice have made all cats escapologists.

Cats have days of melancholy —
and cannot tell you why.

A cat does not speculate about its future. It does not analyze its past. It has no ambitions or regrets. It accepts the moment and makes the best of it.

The world is full of dog lovers.
And cat obsessives.

A cat expects to be adored.

Cats love a game — but expect you to do all the work.

Curious how a newly purchased rug grows steadily more tufty and bald in patches almost overnight. Cat knows the secret.

A sulking cat is solid sulk.

Cats refuse to accept the word
Domesticated.

There are cats who hide in cupboards to avoid visitors. And cats who are downright embarrassing in their efforts to win visitors' hearts.

A happy cat is a reverberating cat.

A kitten can and will fall off almost anything. But will never admit it was an accident.

A cat will vividly enact the chase with a dry leaf as a mouse — until some silly human being says, "Kill it. Kill the mouse!" When he will stare in disdain, "Mouse? For heaven's sake, can't you see it's a dead leaf!"

One has a quite exceptionally clever cat — and one tells one's friends. They come to call — and are confronted by an animal who appears to be not entirely right in the head. It stares at them blankly. "Me? I'm just a poor stupid pussycat." And goes away to laugh in some quiet corner.

Dear Missis, I will love you with at least half my heart. The rest is reserved for the lady next door, who gives me smoked salmon.

People, in exasperation, sometimes wonder whether they own their cats, or their cats own them. The cats do not need to speculate.

Dog and Horse were
seen as Useful and so
were disciplined to fit
Man's needs.
Cat took no notice
and remains simply
and everlastingly
Himself.

Dear cat. I can't switch off the rain.
Forgive me.

Joy is to see a little lost cat ambling up the garden path.

Dear human, you believe you
know what I am thinking
— but you never do.

Every cat is a scrounger
at heart.

It's a hard heart a kitten
cannot melt.

After combing one's cat he seems no thinner, yet one has acquired enough fur to build another cat.

A cat will show its outer beauty to the world and perhaps hint at its affectionate heart. All else is hidden, kept for the one it loves.

Dear cat. You don't do much. You mostly sleep and eat and saunter round the garden. And yet you seem to need my company as I do yours.

The pleasure of living with a cat
is that you never discover
all its secrets.

Every cat needs a window
on the world.

Dog owners prefer certain breeds.
Cat lovers like cats.

Dogs, bless their hearts, are gullible. A cat believes absolutely nothing without proof.

Dogs wait patiently
or otherwise for their masters.
Cats are long gone.

D{ogs} persuade us we are gods. Cats assure us that we are not.

Dogs are loyal. Cats are loyal as long as it suits them.

Every artist and writer needs a cat
companion, critic, inspiration.

Dog whisperers.
Horse whisperers.
But no cat whisperers.

Like flowers, inexhaustible in beauty. Like flowers, most necessary — in ways we scarcely understand. Healers. Companions. Mysteries.

Every cat a critic.

Every cat a tiger in disguise.

The smallest kitten only needs a week to be in full possession of a house and its owners.

A small cat in the window,
a small cat at the door.

And there is love.

Every cat has a secret life.

"Come," says Cat.

"Let's have a scamper."

Every cat knows that the solution to almost everything is sleep.

Every cat is a unique individual.
As are we all.

Every cat needs to be comfortable
— at any cost. It's wonderful how far
a small cat can spread.

A cat has a wild and secretive face,
and the face it shows the
one it loves.

A little cat, a little lonely cat.
Hurt. Afraid.

Astounded by kindness. Rescued.
Safe. A little cat. A little life.

All cats are beautiful

— even the ugly ones.

Every cat is convinced
he knows best.

Every cat owner has the temptation to tie a little purse around their pussy's neck and send it down to the supermarket to choose what it's prepared to eat this week.

I love you. I adore you. You are the center of my life, says Dog.

Of course I love you. Where's dinner? says Cat.

Dogs need to know their place
in The Pack.

Cats haven't the faintest idea
what a Pack is.

Every gesture a cat makes is a
small perfection.

I know my cat loves me
— or I think he does.

Resign yourself.
You can have a cat
or furniture.

His purr overflows his heart
to fill the room.

Dear cats that I have known,
I miss you still, remembering your
eccentricities, your eyes golden
or green, your conversation. You are
the best of all the treasures I have
gathered. I'll hold you safe forever.

Every cat should have a small jungle to explore. Even if it is merely a cabbage patch.

"Fetch, Rover, fetch!" Cat looks on:
"If you want the ball,
you fetch it."

"Get up," says Cat. "Spring has come. Don't let's waste a minute."

Fire, flood, or earthquake. What one treasure would I choose to save? You, of course, dear cat.

A human being is to a cat a scaled-up version of its mother. It cuddles close and accepts her stroking in lieu of its mother's tongue. A kitten still.

Human beings, with patience and tenacity, can be made to understand a cat's demands. Food. Shelter. Comfort. Those who are kind in disposition learn. Those who are not should be abandoned. One can always find another home.

Even a little cat can prove that love
outlasts death.

A cat is mystified when you don't understand his perfectly clear conversation.

Halfway between kitten and cat is katten.

A creature of delight.

A bored cat is an inventive cat.

Buy in bulk the food your cat adores — and be withered with contempt: "That…?"

Every cat — tiger to tabby kitten —
is a masterpiece.

Cats never lose the chance to steal a scene.

One is never bored if one has
a cat about the house.
He sees to that.

Be alert. Your cat can outthink you.

Ask any cat. One does not need opposable thumbs.

Cats are elastic.

Cats know instinctively who
is good at tickling.

Cats are not Almost Human.
They are totally Cat.

Feed me, stroke me, scratch me, says the cat. Arrange amusements.

At last a cat food he's prepared to eat. Buy a case of it. He'll never touch it again.

Anything anti-cat doesn't work.

Cats never perform to order.

Cats know all about cameras.
And which is their
Best Side.

A cat can always manage a second
breakfast — donated by the kind
lady up the road.
Or a third.
Or a fourth.

Any competent psychiatrist confronted with analysis of a feline mind would be driven to retirement after a single session.

A kitten is only a beginning
— a prelude to the glory
of cathood.

Anyone who has a cat suspects
that it is psychic.

Be wary of cute kittens.
They have something
planned.

Watch where you are treading.
I sleep where I want
to sleep.

A cat loves cat toys just so long
as you are prepared to put
in the work.

Even the most affectionate cat needs time to himself. "Of course I love you. Go away."

All cats have a surprise
up their sleeves.

All over the world people are sitting, or lying, in extreme discomfort rather than disturb the cat.

A sleeping cat has discovered
the secret of perfect contentment.

At any moment in time someone on earth is apologizing to a cat.

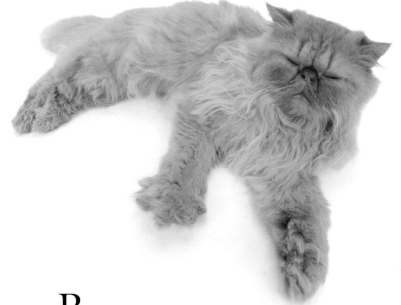

Best ask his owner if you can pet his dog. With cat, ask the cat.

"Tricks? I do tricks.
My own — and when I choose,"
says Cat.

A dog serves. A cat is served.

Preferably with cod.

Every tamed cat is a small,
amiable tyrant.

A cat is a small wild animal
that has chosen
comfort.

Christmas is a time for cats — trees to climb, baubles to bat, soft toys to throttle, cream to lick, turkey to steal. Boxes. Paper. Ribbon. String. And cuddles.

Cats lend us magic and the stuff of dreams.

Cats have made a profession of being adorable. It pays.

Cats never completely leave you. They sidestep Time, shrug off Death — come at the call of memory. Their beauty undiminished. Their touch as gentle. Their love perpetual.

Cats are the superior species.
But have enough sense to keep
quiet about it.

A marvelous pose. Turn. Reach for the camera. Turn back.
He's gone.